Animal Stories 3

For Families

The Science Edition

Collected by Claire Suminski

Illustrated by Susan Swedlund, Pat Mennenger, and Marilyn Miller

Cover Art by Susan Swedlund features Sharon Taylor who was born and raised in the beautiful Burningtown community of Macon County, NC.

Sharon retired from The Mainspring Conservation Trust in February 2020, after joining that non-profit in February of 2001 and then becoming the second director in January of 2015. Her love of this mountain region and its people continue to be reflected in Mainspring's growth and success.

These days you can find Sharon relaxing in her mother, Lucille's, rocker or making her way through the woods with husband, George, celebrating all that nature around her has to offer. She has maintained a healthy respect for millepedes and how they defend themselves! Check out her story on page 5..

First Edition
ISBN 978-1-7374003-3-2

Library of Congress Control Number: 2021945137

Published by Red Press Co.

Redpressco.com

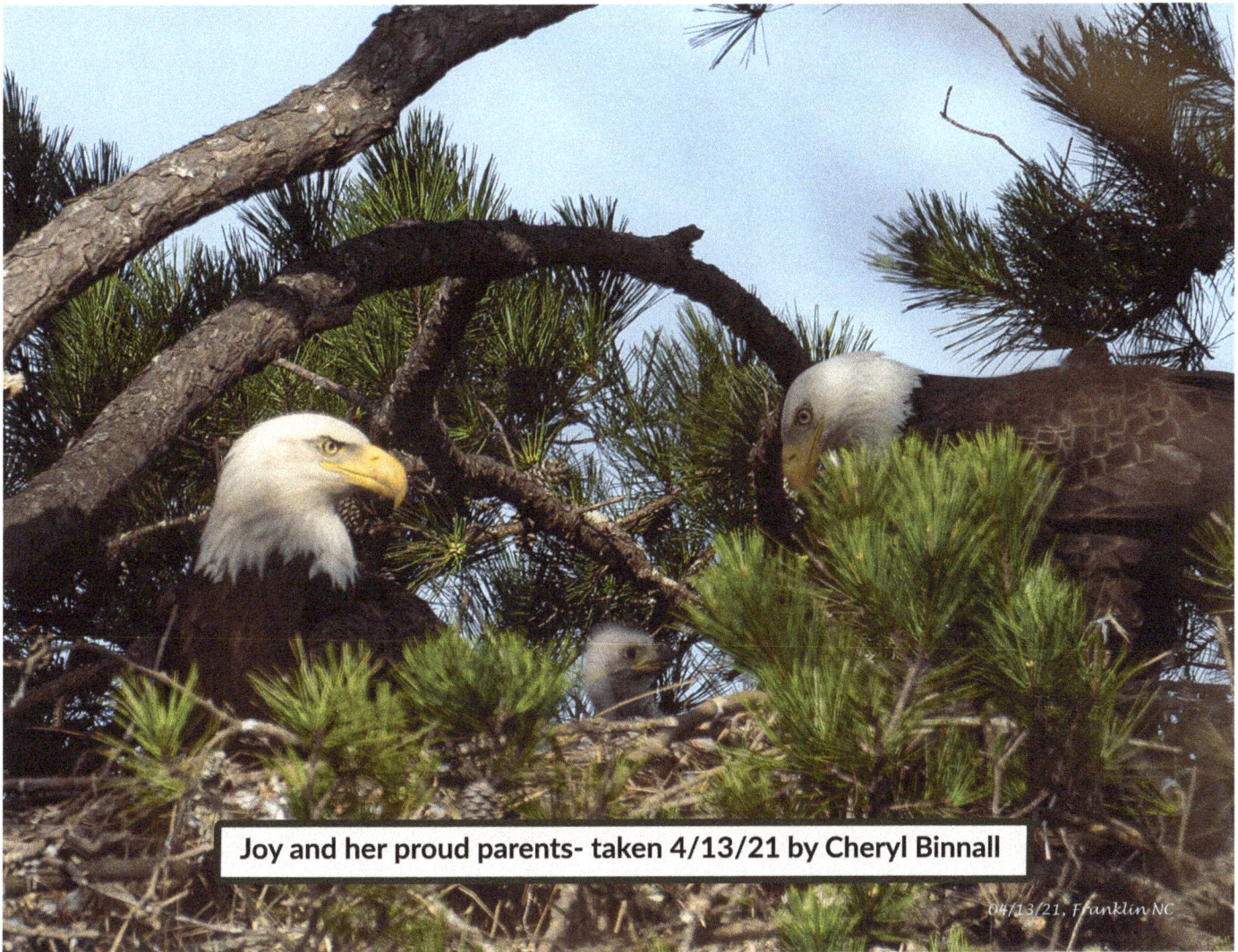

Joy and her proud parents- taken 4/13/21 by Cheryl Binnall

04/13/21, Franklin NC

Back from the brink of extinction, the American Bald Eagle population in our country is now flourishing. In 2017 a pair of bald eagles, "America" and "Bountiful" built a large nest in a tall pine tree near the town of Franklin. Since that time, they have successfully raised 7 baby eaglets!

2018 Courageous and Daring

2019 Freedom and Ernest

2020 Glory and Hallelujah

2021 Joy

Bald eagles mate for life and share in parenting responsibilities. How thrilling it is to watch them soar through the sky as they hunt for food for their young.

20 And God said, Let the waters bring forth abundantly the moving creature that hath life, and fowl [that] may fly above the earth in the open firmament of heaven.

21 And God created great whales, and every living creature that moveth, which the waters brought forth abundantly, after their kind, and every winged fowl after his kind: and God saw that [it was] good.

22 And God blessed them, saying, Be fruitful, and multiply, and fill the waters in the seas, and let fowl multiply in the earth.

23 And the evening and the morning were the fifth day.

24 And God said, Let the earth bring forth the living creature after his kind, cattle, and creeping thing, and beast of the earth after his kind: and it was so.

25 And God made the beast of the earth after his kind, and cattle after their kind, and every thing that creepeth upon the earth after his kind: and God saw that [it was] good.

Genesis 1:20-25 KJV

...and GOD saw that it was good...

Table of Tales

The Science of Animal Defense

CROCODILE

Animals must defend themselves from predators. A predator is an animal that hunts, catches, or eats other animals. So each type of animal has developed methods to defend themselves from harm.

BEAR

Primary Defense:
Make themselves unnoticable by hiding or blending in with their enviroment

CAT

Secondary Defenses:

Running away

DOG

Distracting methods like making a sound, putting off a scent, or by squirting or spitting at the threat

Playing dead so that the predator loses interest

DINGO

Banding together with their group to form a sheild or appear to be a threat to the predator

MOOSE

Posturing, or making themselves appear bigger than they really are to cause the predator to pause and reconsider its attack

COW

A Day at the Zoo

By Pat Mennenger

Lowry Park Zoo is located in the heart of the city of Tampa, Florida. Most of the time being a docent there was enjoyable, but one day turned out to be anything but that.

It was a hot summer day when I picked up my badge at the front office. A gentle ocean breeze rustled the leaves of the banana trees that lined the walkway into the zoo. Children were laughing and splashing in the fountains at the entrance. I could hear the calls of monkeys and parrots while the smell of popcorn and fresh hay filled the air.

My job that day was to talk to visitors and tell them about the animals. A small crowd had gathered at the llama enclosure. Everyone listened intently as I told them that we called the girl llama Mabelline because she looked like she had mascara on her beautiful lashes. The boy llama's name was Argyle because his legs had diamond shaped markings that looked like argyle socks.

While talking, I bent down to point at his legs. As I stood up the last thing I saw was his lips flutter. Then everything went black.

Argyle had spit the contents of his stomach right in my face! (When llamas are alarmed, they react by spitting and always aim for your eyes.) My glasses were covered with chewed grass and corn and the whole mess was dripping off my chin and running down inside the front of my shirt. There was even some in my mouth. It smelled like you-know-what. That's right, puke!

That was the end of my talk that day. I ran all the way to the bathroom to get cleaned up.

Later I was telling the zoo's curator about my encounter with Argyle. There was a pause and he said, "Have you ever seen a camel spit? You'll need a shovel."

In Defense of a Millipede

By Sharon Taylor

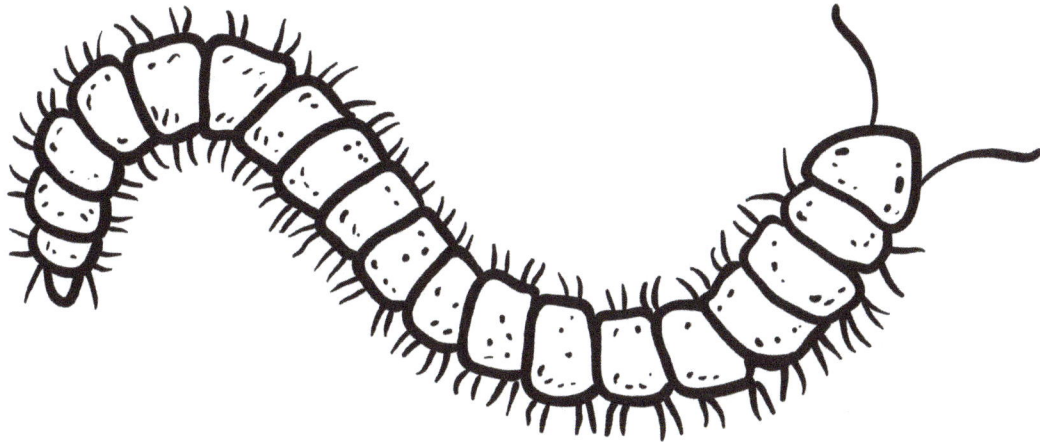

Studying biology made me curious about all forms of life, so much so, that one day I picked up a long millipede crawling along a wooded hiking trail. When I started the hike that day, I knew a few things about millipedes. I knew they were scavengers and ate damp wood bits and leaves. I knew they had an effective defense system of coiling into a ball and could emit a toxin to keep predators like spiders and ants away, and I also knew they had dozens of paired legs.

Their legs were what was on my mind as I reached down and picked the millipede up from the trail. But alas, before I could get to look at its legs, the millipede spayed an almond smelling liquid directly onto my face, landing mostly on my mouth. My lips and skin began to burn and blister immediately. Was I shocked! I've since read that some large millipedes can spray their toxins up to 32 inches.

Amazing!

I survived the rash and can only hope the millipede survived its quick trip back to the trail.

5

CROCODILE

BEAR

CAT

DOG

DINGO

MOOSE

COW

THE SCIENCE OF ANIMAL SCENT

Science has found that most animals have a sense of smell, but the organ they use to smell can differ wildly from one animal to the next. Each basic category of animal has its own unique way of smelling. For instance, amphibians like frogs use nares, which are holes starting in the mouth and leading to the face, like human nostrils. Fish also use nares, taking in water that moves over sensory pads in their heads that tell their brains what they are smelling. Birds smell through nostrils found on their beaks. Mammal nostrils, on the other hand, are located on the nose. Mammals have a large range of smell, and some are better at it than others. Dogs, for example, are very good at sniffing, while elephants are even better; both of them can smell better than humans can.

Insects use receptors on their bodies that contain pores, or holes, that pick up scents from the air. Reptiles like lizards are even more unusual because they use their tongue to smell. They flick their tongue to pick up scent particles from the air, and when their tongue goes back into their mouth, it rests on the roof of the mouth, where special sensors interpret the scent.

Leanna Serras
https://www.fragrancex
.com/fragrance-informa
tion/how-do-animals-u
se-smalls.htm

Snakes smell with their tongues. They rely heavily on their sense of smell because they have a limited ability to see or hear.

Dogs can smell somewhere between 10,000 to 100,000 times better than humans. Also, the part of a dog's brain that is devoted to analyzing smells is about 40 times greater than ours!

Bears have a super strong sense of smell and are considered to have the greatest sense of smell of all mammals. They can smell things from a mile away!

"Bear"—Ly Awake

As told to Claire Suminski by Taylor Earman

I live and work in Highlands, North Carolina. In fact I have 2 jobs. Some days I work both jobs, which makes me especially tired. One day I worked all day at my landscaping job and then went right to my second job at the Lakeside Restaurant washing dishes. When my shift was over, I could hardly wait to get home and relax out on the deck of my apartment, which is right off the Franklin Highway, that goes down through the Cullasaja Gorge to Franklin. I live near the Bascom Center for the Visual Arts, and only a stone's throw from the Highlands Smokehouse.

That night, when I arrived home, I was too tired to take a shower and wash all the sweat and food smells off. Instead, I grabbed an ice cold drink from the fridge and headed for the deck. The patio furniture on the deck looked very inviting and so I took a long swig of my drink and made myself comfortable on the chaise lounge. The wonderful scent of smoke house barbecue greeted my nostrils, but I was too tired to think about eating. Before I knew it, the mountain sounds and cool evening breeze had lulled me to sleep. Ah, rest at last!

Then, floating in a dream like state, I had the sensation of what seemed like wet kisses peppering my cheek. I reached through the fog of sleep trying to figure this out; after all, I thought I was all alone. As, I started to wake up, I realized my cheek was being licked vigorously. My eyelids flew open and I was staring into the mouth of a very large black Mama bear! My heart was racing! Was I on the menu for this bear's next meal? She had me pinned in the chaise lounge and I could not get up. I was breathing hard, but could not get any sound to come out of my mouth! And then, the bear seemed to lose interest, stopped licking me and ambled down the deck stairs and into the woods.

It is common knowledge in our neighborhood, that bears come out of the woods to try and raid the dumpster at the smokehouse. It must smell so good to them! In the next few weeks, the Mama bear came back to visit me and brought her two young cubs. But I made a lot of noise and flailed my arms to keep them moving and then watched them from inside my apartment. I know that it is not safe for the bears or for me to try and make friends with them.

I try to shower right after work now, and tend to take naps in the living room instead of on the deck. After all, even though this has made a very interesting story, I don't plan on waking up again, being licked by a mama bear!

Cousins from New York
Wesser Bald Hike October

Joe and Annie
Wesser Bald Hike– October

Max's Wesser Bald Adventure

Appalachian Trail, Nantahala Forest, Western North Carolina

By Claire Suminski

Acrylic Paintings by Marilyn Miller

I grew up at the foot of the Adirondack Mountains in upstate New York. My Dad wanted to retire in a similar place, but with winters that were less extreme. He moved to Franklin with his devoted canine companion, Max. My husband Joe, our young daughter Annie and I soon followed. I moved to Franklin sight unseen, but when we made the descent, down Cowee Mountain, Southwest on 441, I knew I was home!

Wesser Bald Fire Tower is 30 feet tall and has a spectacular 360 degree view of the Nantahala and Smoky Mountains. The summit at the base of the tower is 4,627 feet. One beautiful Fall day, during a visit from our upstate New York family, we decided to head North of Franklin through the Tellico Valley in order to make the 4 mile roundtrip hike to Wesser Bald. My Dad decided to bring his dog, Max, who rarely left his side. We made it up to the tower and enjoyed a late lunch while taking in the incredible 360 degree view. As the afternoon shadows began to fall and the children grew tired, we headed back down the path. Half way back to the gravel road, Max's ears perked up and his nose started twitching; he took off like a rocket! My Dad, who had a very high estimation of Max's nose, said not to worry, that he was sure Max would be back. It took us another 30 minutes to reach the parking area, as the sun was setting over the Western ridge. Max was no where to be found. While the rest of us loaded into our cars, my Father and husband hiked back up the trail a little ways, calling and whistling for Max. Where could he be?

Lunch Break
Wesser Bald Hike October

Dad and the cousins making their
way down from the top

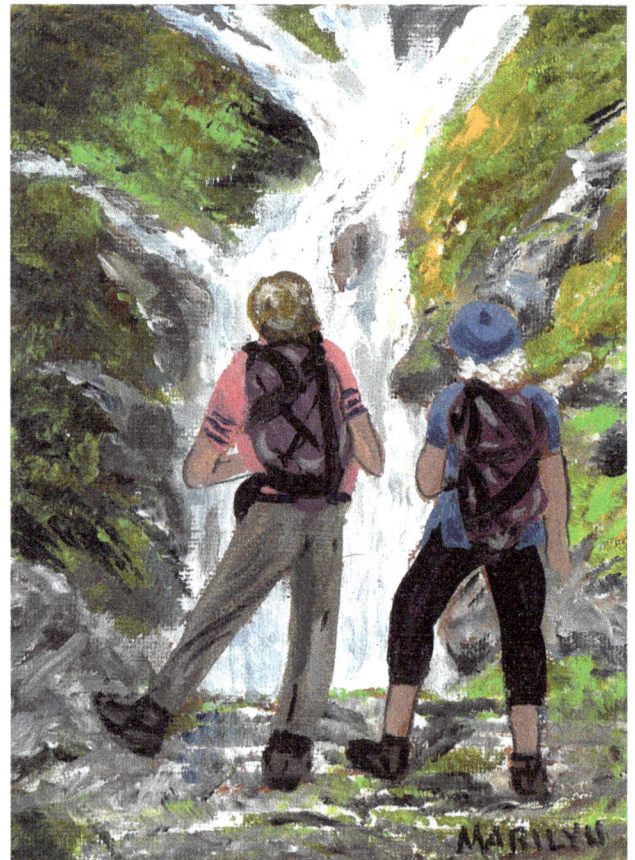

Enjoying the view of the Falls
Wesser Bald Hike

Joe and Anne
Wesser Bald Hike October

Back at the parking area, it was decision time. The sun had set and we needed to head back down Tellico Road. Knowing that there were bears and wild boars and other critters that Max might get tangled up with during the night, our family gathered and prayed for his safety. Then my Dad did something quite unusual. He took off his trousers and made an oval nest out of them on the edge of the parking lot. We quietly climbed in our car, my Dad in his boxer shorts, and headed back down through Tellico Valley, a small group of us planning to return at sunrise.

The next morning we got up, brewed some coffee and headed back North through Tellico Valley again, continuing to pray for Max's return. We expected he would be there. As we pulled into the parking area, the first thing I saw was a tail wagging quickly, floppy ears perking up and even what appeared to be a big dog smile on Max's face. He was sitting right on top of Dad's pants! My Father's voice was husky and there were tears in his eyes as he opened the door and called Max's name. Max ran as fast as his short legs would take him and put his paws on Dad's knees, giving Dad a good chance to check him over for injuries. Not a scratch was on him.

Max had found the scent of my Dad and spent the coldest hours of the night curled up on his pants. It was a joyous reunion! His powerful nose had showed him the way.

We had deep gratitude for this wonderful answer to prayer!

Brain Freeze

as told to Claire Suminski by Taylor Earman

This is another story from one of Highland's hard working citizens. He is a landscaper by day and dish washer by night, Taylor Earman.

Taylor was working on some Spring landscaping up in the wild and beautiful Horse Cove area of Highlands, on a piece of property that butts up against the incredible stone formation called Black Rock. Many of Taylor's customers have him dig up their Dahlias for the winter and re-plant them in the Spring. One beautiful Spring day as he was replanting Dahlias for one of his favorite customers, he noticed that a big black mama bear was lumbering around the property. He was a little concerned, but kept working. If the bear came close he would stand up and wave his arms and holler and the bear would retreat to the woods.

As the afternoon wore on, the bear was becoming bolder and made a dash for the open door of the garage. Taylor was hollering and the man of the house came out on the porch to see what the ruckus was. This big Mama bear, had opened up the chest freezer and was rooting around inside. The owner yelled in his very Southern Alabama accent, "Why she must be after my wife's 25 pound bag of Alabama shrimp!" And sure enough, she was. He grabbed his shotgun and fired it into the air. The bear grabbed her bounty and took off for the edge of the woods. Even though it was about $250 worth of shrimp, both the owner and Taylor thought it not wise to try and get it away from Mama.

As Taylor watched, the bear tore open the bag with her teeth and gobbled down piece after piece of the frozen solid extra large Alabama shrimp. Next thing he knew, she was dancing around and rubbing the side of her head with her paw. He hollered out to the bear, "That's right, Mama, you've got brain freeze!" She ran off into the woods and Taylor thought for a minute that he might go and retrieve what was left. But while he was still deciding, back out of the woods came Mama with two bear cubs. The shrimp had thawed a little more by that time and they settled in for a feast. Mama bear turned and looked back at her benefactor's home, as if to say, "We love us some Alabama shrimp! Thank you!"

CROCODILE

BEAR

CAT

DOG

DINGO

MOOSE

COW

THE SCIENCE OF ENVIRONMENTAL EFFECTS

The environment includes the living and nonliving things that animals and organisms interact with in their habitat. At times an environment will be effected by the actions of man. Forest fires, pollution, clearing and building on once wild land can and does effect the behavior of animals. So occasionally you will find animals such as deer, bear, and coyotes in places normally they would not be - like your backyard!

When the Deer Came Down

As told to Claire Suminski by Dave Barlow

My friend Dave and his wife, Donna, used to live in a log style cabin on Brendle Road, right at the bottom of old Coon Creek Road, located on the East side of the town of Franklin. Brendle Road is shaped like a horseshoe with hills and mountains on three sides.

In the Fall of 2016 Western Carolina was besieged by over 33 fires covering over 40,000 acres. The smoke rolled down into the valleys, mixing with the regular mountain mist. This affected humans and animals, decreasing visibility and making it harder to breath at times.

One November evening, during these fires, Dave went out to putter in his maintenance shed. This mixture of mist and smoke had settled into his yard and the neighboring field, right across Coon Creek. It was very quiet, but suddenly, Dave heard what sounded like hooves clomping in this gravel driveway right outside his shed. As he stepped through the doorway to investigate, a gust of wind blew the smoke and mist further down Brendle Road and he saw an amazing site.

Dave estimates that a herd of over 70 deer had come down out of the mountains and were grazing in his yard and the field. The greatest concentration seemed to be eating the wind fallen apples on the ground around a large apple tree in the center of the field. Normally, he might see 4 or 5 deer in his neighborhood. This time there were deer spread out as far as he could see. The fires seemed to have brought them down into the valley. To this day, Dave has never seen that many deer together.

THE SCIENCE OF ANIMAL INSTINCT

CROCODILE

BEAR

CAT

DOG

DINGO

MOOSE

COW

All animals with nervous systems have instincts, or behaviors, that occur when triggered by certain stimuli. They are not learned behaviors but inherited automatic reactions.

Newly hatched Sea Turtles on a beach will automatically move toward the ocean and instinctively know how to swim.

Cats instictively know that mice are prey and will chase after them with barely a thought.

A Crash Course In Swimming

By Mardi White

When my "Golden Years" sweetheart, Ron, and I combined our canine families, some new dog relationships were formed. Our two largest dogs, Pax, who was a Chocolate/Labrador Retriever and Joey, a shepherd/Labrador mix, became the best of friends. Joey was quite a swimmer and enjoyed his dips in the lake every time we took a walk but we wondered about Pax. She loved the water, but we never saw her feet leave the bottom. We just assumed she did not know how to swim. Since Pax was a Retriever, we really hoped that someday we would see her paddle through the water!

One day, we took Pax and Joey to Lake Chattooga, in Hiawassee, GA for some off leash trail walking. The dogs were busily sniffing and exploring the surrounding forest, when a large buck darted across the trail ahead of us. Pax must have picked up the scent of that deer because she made a bee line toward the surprised buck. The deer took off running toward the lake with Pax giving chase. Before we knew it, Joey had noticed the action and joined Pax in hot pursuit. And then with a splash, all three were in the water.

Ron and I stood on the shoreline for 20 minutes, watching our dogs swimming right on the heels of that big buck. The deer stayed just far enough ahead to keep the dogs focused. The three continued all the way across Lake Chattooga. From our vantage point, their heads looked like little ping pong balls, bobbing in the water.

Finally, we saw the deer reach the far shore. Pax gave up the chase and turned back, swimming the long distance back to our shore. But where was Joey? Through Ron's binoculars, we had seen Joey disappear behind an island. Where could he be? After allowing Pax to rest, we headed down the trail towards the car to make our way around the lake to the far shore. But as Ron and I hurried along the trail, we could not believe our eyes. Up ahead, standing on the trail was Joey, acting as if he had been waiting for us to catch up with him! He had found his way back. This story has always amazed us and we were so thankful that we did not lose Joey, but now we know one thing for sure...

Those dogs can swim!

what a Fellowship

by Claire Suminski

We have hosted many events on our small family farm where the Little Tennessee River flows into Lake Emory, near the base of Cowee Mountain, just outside of Franklin, NC. A couple of years ago we were having a Spring Bible weekend on the grounds, with the main meeting area set up in a tent overlooking the pasture next to the lake. It was such a beautiful Spring day. The sun shining, the birds singing and the flowers were blooming. We were singing in the tent,

"What a fellowship, what a joy divine, leaning on the everlasting arms."

I saw a text from our neighbor, Rose, coming through on my cell phone and glanced down to see if it needed immediate attention. She was sitting on her porch, over looking the lake, and humming along to with the music,

"O how bright the path grows from day to day, leaning on the everlasting arms."

She saw a large black dog jump out of the bushes on the edge of the pasture below the meeting tent. It started to swim across the lake almost to the beat of the music.

"Leaning, leaning, leaning on the everlasting arms."

It was an unusual site, so Rose said she was making a video for us to watch later. When we broke for lunch, I heard a ping on my phone and saw that the video had come through, with a comment..... "You are not going to believe this! Enlarge screen for better view." I pushed play and made the screen bigger. There, swimming across the lake only a short distance from where we were singing was not a big black dog, but a big black bear!

23

The bear was swimming almost to the beat of the music, while we were,

" Leaning, Leaning, Leaning on the everlasting arms."

What a fellowship!

WHEN SCIENCE RELATES TO HABITAT AND WILDLIFE ASSISTANCE

CROCODILE

BEAR

CAT

DOG

DINGO

MOOSE

COW

Good stewardship of natural habitat and care of injured and orphaned animals are two ways people help wildlife. The next three stories are examples of Zoologists, Biologists, Hydrologists, and other trained employees and volunteers working within organizations to provide help.

Since 1997, Mainspring Conservation Trust has been dedicated to three core initiatives in the heart of the Southern Blue Ridge: conserve the land, restore the water and connect the people to these valuable resources. Dr William McLarney is an award-winning Aquatic Conservation Biologist who has directed a biomonitoring of the upper Little Tennessee watershed for over 30 years. He works with Mainspring's Biomonitoring Program, which is one of the most successful in North America. Mainspring's vision is clean water flowing through a healthy, rural landscape and a vibrant, sustainable economy within a well-functioning ecosystem. Their land conservation efforts and educational outreach programs are helping greatly in land stewardship and preservation of natural habitats.

The Milwaukee County Zoo supports and participates in global conservation of animal species and their environment. They contribute to worldwide animal management, conservation and research efforts. They also act as wildlife ambassadors in hopes that those that visit their zoo will be "motivated to join them in taking action to protect and preserve wildlife."

The Tampa Zoo (from section one in this book) has a similar mission: To rescue, rehabilitate and care for animals; and create exceptional personalized experiences that connect people with wildlife and each other in fun, immersive ways.

The International Primate Protection League (IPPL) is a grassroots nonprofit organization whose mission has been rescuing and helping exploited primates, great and small, from around the world since 1973. Their Gibbon sanctuary is located in South Carolina and is also home to the Asian Otters in this book. IPPL supports primate rescue efforts worldwide, especially in countries where these animals are native.

Milwaukee County Zoo

Animal Stories

Suzy, the Sweet Siamang

As told to Claire Suminski by Jane Suminski

Our cousin, Jane worked for The Milwaukee County Zoo for several years. This zoo covers 190 acres and houses 1800 animals. During Jane's time at the Milwaukee Zoo, she especially enjoyed helping to care for a Siamang named Suzy.

Siamangs are endangered primates that inhabit the Malay peninsula and the monsoon forests of Indonesia, Malaysia and Thailand. Suzy was brought to the US as part of the illegal pet trade and ended up at the Milwaukee Zoo. Suzy and her mate, Unk, enjoyed many years together at the zoo. Suzy was known for her sweet disposition but Unk was rough around the edges. After Unk died, Cousin Jane spent more time caring for Suzy and shared some fond memories. Suzy was supposed to be brushed regularly. When Jane would enter her area to take care of her, Suzy would stick out one limb at a time for Jane to brush. One day, when Jane was through, Suzy wrapped her freshly brushed big ape arms around her and gave her a hug! That put a big smile on Jane's face.

27

Mother's in captivity do not always take to mothering their young. There was a Spider Monkey named Gomez who was rejected by his mother at birth. In fact, his mother left him under a drainage pipe to die. Suzy had successfully raised babies before and the zoo keepers decided to try and put Gomez with Suzy. That was a great idea and it saved this young spider monkey's life. Suzy cared for Gomez so well and would bring him to the caretakers at feeding time for him to get his bottle, since she had no milk. When he was grown and ready to be on his own, he went to another zoo and it became clear that he was different than most spider monkeys. Gomez was a spider monkey that moved and acted like a Siamang Ape. Suzy in all her Siamang mothering ways had imprinted herself permanently on Gomez!

Jane went on to become a Science teacher in the Milwaukee County Schools, but still fondly remembers and misses the animals at the zoo, especially Suzy the sweet Siamang Ape.

MEET
CRYPTOBRANCHUS ALLEGANIENSIS

Artwork is from a original photo by Fabiana Silva

Dr. Bill McLarney hails from upstate New York and remembers finding *Cryptobranchus alleganiensis*, Latin name for the Eastern Hellbender, in northern streams, as a boy. An award-winning Aquatic Conservation Biologist, who now resides in the Oak Grove Community of Macon County, Bill oversees the Biomonitoring Program at Mainspring Conservation Trust, headquartered in Franklin, North Carolina. In this program, which surveys the upper Little Tennessee watershed, the main focus is sampling fish assemblages. But through the years of leading groups in stream biomonitoring, the survey team has come face to face with many Eastern Hellbenders. Bill shares his findings with Lori Williams, the North Carolina Wildlife Commission's Wildlife Diversity Biologist who specializes in studying hellbenders. Lori, is very interested in tracking the life and habits of this elusive giant aquatic salamander. Hellbenders are listed as a "species of special concern" in North Carolina and are considered indicators of water quality.

29

Eastern Hellbender

Snot Otter

Lasagna Lizard

Alleghany Alligator

CRYPTOBRANCHUS ALLEGANIENSIS

Running across one of these amphibians in a river or stream may seem like a step back in time. Flat bodied with short limbs, small eyes and a coating of slime, the Eastern Hellbender, has an archaic look. This can cause a first time encounter to result in an exclamation of "What is this?!" Bill is used to hearing remarks like that and is grateful whenever one of these giant salamanders is seen during the biomonitoring process. This unusual looking stream dweller has earned some very interesting nicknames: most commonly, Snot Otter, Lasagna Lizard and Alleghany Alligator.

The hellbender breathes through its skin and that is why this species is a very good indicator of water quality. Hellbenders spend their whole lives in the water and can be found mostly in spaces under rocks. These amphibians breathe through pores found in their fleshy folds resembling lasagna noodles, which is what earned them the nickname "Lasagna Lizards"! Chemicals used in farming and silt from construction run off, affect the quality of water and can make it hard for them to breathe or even survive. This is why Eastern Hellbenders are an indicator species for the state of streams and the importance of clean water habitat for wildlife.

The nickname "Snot Otter" came about because of the mucus covering this amphibian's skin, which protects it from predators and disease. This giant salamander can reach up to 29 inches in length, but is harmless to people. It lives mostly under rock overhangs, making it seem even more elusive. Sightings often happen when the Alleghany Alligator comes out from underneath his rock in search of food. People moving big rocks in streams can cause damage to hellbenders and other "under rock shelf dwellers".

For several years, Bill noticed that the Eastern Hellbender population was declining. In the years from 2015 to 2018 his team had no sightings during their biomonitoring. But then, one was seen in 2019 and another two in 2021. There is much work to be done in the field of watershed restoration. But Bill is hopeful that as the water quality in the upper Little Tennessee watershed improves, these wonderful aquatic salamanders will again flourish in these mountains.

More information :Chattanooga Zoo Hiwassee Hellbender Research, lori.williams@ncwildlife.org, or Kimberly Terrell/Smithsonian Hellbender

Raising Otter Triplets

by Allison Harvey

I was a surrogate mother to three orphaned, Asian small-clawed otter pups, born in captivity at IPPL's headquarters* on May 13th, 1988. Peggy, their biological mother, produced numerous healthy litters with Ottie, her life-long mate at the sanctuary. Now Peggy was a senior and, although she survived giving birth to triplets, she developed pneumonia and died when her pups were only two weeks old. Chunky, Jerry and Gloria were easily distinguishable from the beginning. Chunky was plump, hence his name, and took to the bottle enthusiastically. Jerry was the "runt of the litter," and I constantly fretted about him. Gloria, bright-eyed and alert, was an average newborn but eventually surpassed Chunky in size and weight.

I was a member of a rotating team of three volunteer round-the-clock caregivers. We quickly implemented a feeding schedule. I worked the "night shift" and took the pups home. Accepting responsibility for the vulnerable trio, members of an endangered species native to South and Southeast Asia, was a dream come true. The Asian Small Clawed Otter, also called the Asian Short Clawed Otter, is the world's smallest of the thirteen otter species. A semiaquatic animal, its fleshy, semi-webbed paws resemble childlike human hands, dexterous enough to grasp small fish and shellfish to feed on. I had never seen such stunning baby animals in my life.

Being alone with them that first night was daunting, but my maternal instincts kicked in, and I was determined the pups would thrive on my watch. Bottle-babies can decline rapidly after a bout of diarrhea. Dehydration, aspiration, and pneumonia are all serious concerns, especially for exotic and wild animals. I kept a journal, moved from master bedroom to guest room, equipped myself with an alarm clock, cardboard box, hand towels, washcloths, heating pad, kitchen scale, special veterinarian recommended formula for otter pups, tiny bottles and nipples that I sterilized after every feeding, and my treasured coffee mug. The amounts of formula the pups drank increased with every ounce they gained. They stretched their bodies while nursing and "paw kneaded" the air. They squealed when hungry, burped when full, and even got the hiccups. I observed every sound and movement they made with awe. I especially loved watching them dream. Their supple bodies twitched, and they whistled faintly. Were they remembering their mother Peggy? The babies thrived as they transitioned from bottle to pulverized food on a plate.

33

Soon our team was working together during the day, teaching them how to swim and grasp solid food with their rubbery paws. Gloria engaged in "play-fights" with her brothers. She was quite a tease, and so bossy that we referred to her as the "sassy sister". Another volunteer duty was swimming instructor. Baby otters cannot swim, they have to be tutored by their mothers. So, we volunteers had to give swimming lessons to our little otters!

The three lived long, happy lives. Never has there been quite the anticipation and excitement within the otter community at IPPL as there was during the months after Chunky, Jerry and Gloria arrived. Peggy and Ottie's last litter, a legacy of precious memories, is cherished in my heart forever.

*Many thanks to Allison Harvey and the IPPL Board of Directors for allowing us to reprint this article from their Fall 2020 Newsletter.

For more information, contact them at info@ippl.org or visit their Facebook page: www.facebook.com/ InternationalPrimateProtectionLeague

Experiment and Explore

Animal Track Action!

First we Experiment:
What types of soil make the best animal track imprints?

You will need:
*5 cups or more of sand
*5 cups or more of potting soil or sifted soil from your garden
*4 flat containers
*Towel (to dry your hands in between imprints)
*Spray bottle of water (to wet trays 2 and 4 and to wash hands)

Set up:

Tray 1	Tray 2	Tray 3	Tray 4
Dry Sand	Wet Sand	Dry Soil	Wet Soil

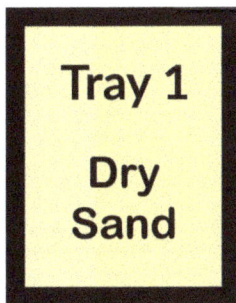

Use a spray bottle to wet the sand in tray 2 and the soil in tray 4. You want them wet but not flooded with water.

Develop a Hypothesis:
A hypothesis is your best guess as to what will occur in your experiment. You are going to make a handprint in each tray. Which pan will show and keep your handprint the best? Why do you think so?

Procedure:
(Make sure your hand is clean and dry before setting it in each tray.)

1- Press the palm of your hand and fingers firmly into tray 1, then wash and dry your hand. Repeat for trays 2-4.

2-Which tray has the best imprint of your hand?

3- Was your hypothesis correct?

4- What did you learn? With this new knowledge, where do you think you could find and see animal tracks near where you live?

Now it is time to explore!

Along with your parents or an adult take a hike along a river or lake front and look for animal tracks. Use the dichotomous key on the next page to help identify the tracks you are seeing.

A dichotomous key is a tool that helps the user determine the identity of items in nature, such as trees, wildflowers, mammals, reptiles, rocks, and fish. Keys consist of a series of choices that lead the user to the correct name of a given item.

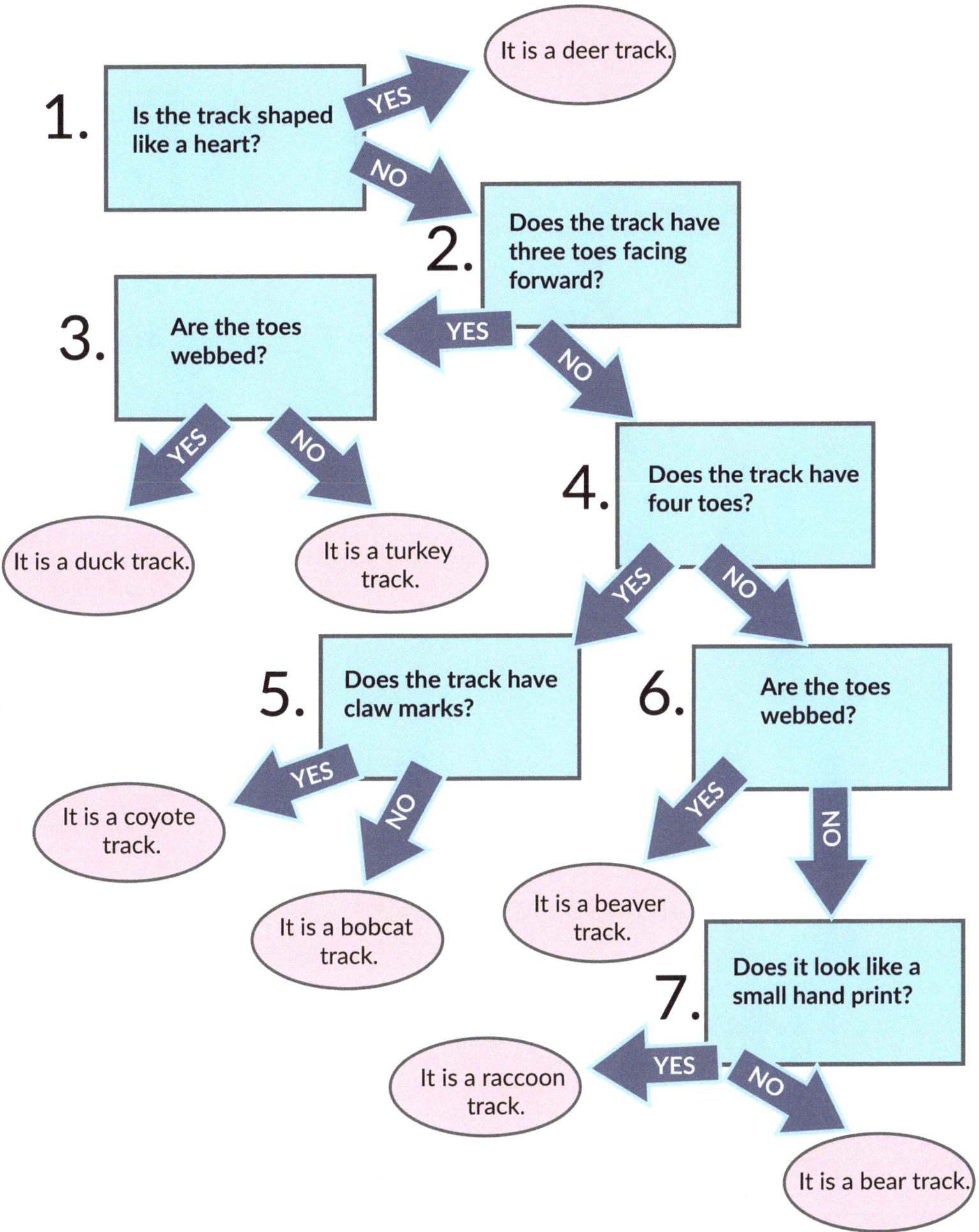

1. Is the track shaped like a heart?

- **YES** → It is a deer track.
- **NO** → **2.** Does the track have three toes facing forward?

2. Does the track have three toes facing forward?

- **YES** → **3.** Are the toes webbed?
- **NO** → **4.** Does the track have four toes?

3. Are the toes webbed?

- **YES** → It is a duck track.
- **NO** → It is a turkey track.

4. Does the track have four toes?

- **YES** → **5.** Does the track have claw marks?
- **NO** → **6.** Are the toes webbed?

5. Does the track have claw marks?

- **YES** → It is a coyote track.
- **NO** → It is a bobcat track.

6. Are the toes webbed?

- **YES** → It is a beaver track.
- **NO** → **7.** Does it look like a small hand print?

7. Does it look like a small hand print?

- **YES** → It is a raccoon track.
- **NO** → It is a bear track.

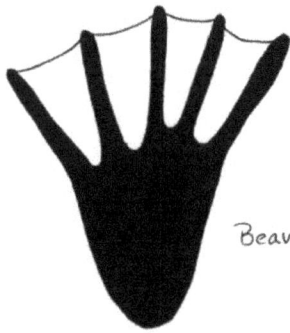

Beaver

Raccoon

Deer

Duck

Black Bear

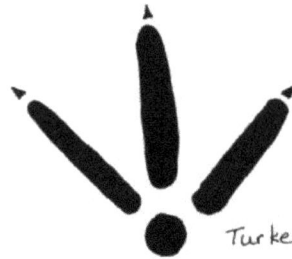

Turkey

Coyote

Bobcat

ROOSTER	GOOSE	DOVE	TURKEY	DUCK	HEN	OSTRICH	CROCODILE
RACOON	MOLE	HEDGEHOG	KOALA	SQUIRREL	LEMUR	BEAVER	BEAR
ECHIDNA	GORILLA	LION	MINK	FOX	CARACAL	WOLF	CAT
TIGER	MEERKAT	HYENA	CHEETAH	BADGER	LYNX	RABBIT	DOG
ELEPHANT	ZEBRA	TAPIR	WILD BOAR	RHINO	COATI	LEOPARD	DINGO
GIRAFFE	IMPALA	SPRINGBOK	HIPPO	LLAMA	HORSE	DONKEY	MOOSE
ROE	DUIKER	OKAPI	DEER	PIG	GOAT	SHEEP	COW

ANIMAL SCIENCE PUZZLE

Find and circle the words from the list below. You will find the words going across, up & down and diagonal.

```
I  B  T  M  X  Z  X  Y  P  M  J  A  K  S  S  J  H  C  S  C
E  U  U  Z  R  D  M  X  R  X  I  D  N  U  D  Y  Z  U  C  R
H  N  Z  U  H  V  O  I  I  D  S  L  J  K  E  F  I  R  I  C
O  Y  S  T  S  B  N  T  M  P  N  S  L  R  E  I  L  A  E  O
T  L  R  B  P  Y  K  L  A  U  I  O  I  I  R  P  J  T  N  T
H  H  N  Y  R  V  E  T  T  K  G  F  S  H  P  U  C  O  C  E
Y  C  E  N  C  Y  Y  I  E  T  W  Z  W  M  A  E  P  R  E  L
P  C  V  U  K  O  H  R  S  U  B  G  I  S  I  C  D  S  C  L
B  J  N  A  T  H  B  V  S  J  L  V  S  M  N  Q  A  E  V  A
C  J  W  N  P  S  M  E  I  B  F  Z  H  N  S  C  P  V  G  M
O  L  A  I  R  Z  H  A  A  P  T  S  E  D  T  U  V  T  X  A
T  B  M  M  D  S  Y  C  M  R  U  H  L  P  I  S  R  U  D  N
T  R  D  A  F  C  U  I  A  Q  H  A  L  H  N  H  X  G  E  B
E  H  Z  L  U  E  P  U  N  B  H  B  B  D  C  R  E  A  F  X
R  U  W  E  D  N  Z  C  G  N  I  I  E  T  T  I  M  C  E  V
C  C  Q  B  Y  T  A  G  U  K  L  T  N  G  W  M  H  A  N  C
Y  P  S  W  I  M  M  I  N  G  N  A  D  R  K  P  U  N  S  I
Z  M  F  I  P  T  K  P  B  M  O  T  E  O  U  S  B  I  E  T
O  B  A  B  I  E  S  K  V  U  S  B  R  O  J  F  E  N  T  F
O  J  C  T  C  B  L  W  I  L  D  L  I  F  E  T  E  E  N  M
```

HELLBENDER	MILLIPEDE	INSTINCT	SWIMMING
PRIMATES	WILDLIFE	CURATOR	DEFENSE
SIAMANG	HABITAT	SCIENCE	MONKEY
ANIMAL	CANINE	SHRIMP	BABIES
SCENT	LLAMA	BEAR	OTTER
DEER	ZOO		

The answers can be found in the back of this book.

Animal Science
Word Scramble

Unscramble the words below. The first three are warm-ups. If you need some clues look below.

1. LLAAM

2. TROET

3. BERA

4. YLIGOOB

5. CRVGNESEAS

6. CTESN

7. NRNNEVOIMET

8. IITSNTNC

9. BTAIHAT

10. ILIFWEDL

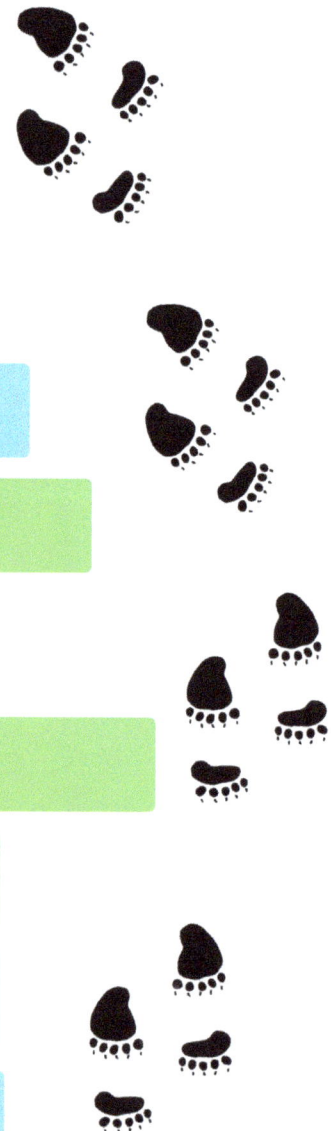

If you need some clues search these pages.
1-pg.1, 2-pg.33, 3-pg.8, 4-pg.5, 5-pg.5, 6-pg.6, 7-pg.16,
8-pg.19, 9-pg.25, 10-pg.25

The answers can be found in the back of this book.

Many thanks to all who shared their stories in this book: Pat, Sharon, Taylor, Dave, Mardi, Jane, Bill and Allison. We would also like to thank our proofreader, Kelli Kurczewski.

Meet Lead Author and Storyteller: Claire Suminski

Claire enjoys collecting stories from family members, friends and from her travels. She often remarks that God made all of the different animals, not man, and what what an amazing job He did! Claire was raised in the Adirondack region of New York. She and her husband, Joe, moved to Western North Carolina in 1991. The Suminski Family enjoys their small working farm, which is nestled in a peaceful mountain valley along the Little Tennessee River. Writing stories that awaken wonder in the hearts of children, brings her great joy.

Meet the Illustrators : Susan Swedlund, Pat Mennenger & Marilyn Miller

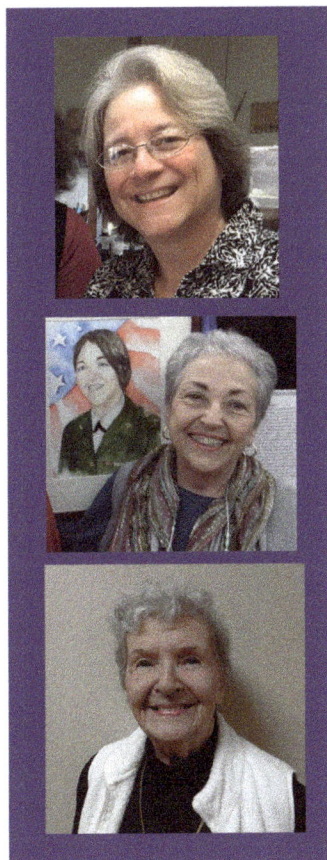

Susan is a multi-media artist. She works as a graphic artist for Suminski Family Books, does open air water color painting and works with clay. She loves making ceramic pieces and teaching others the fundamentals of working with clay. While Susan and her husband reside in Beloit, Wisconsin, they enjoy spending a portion of the year in Franklin, North Carolina. Susan's illustrative work can be seen on pages 4, 17-18, 20-24, 26-31.

Pat wrote and illustrated *"A Day at the Zoo"* (pg.2), and illustrated *"Bear-ly Awake"* (pg.8 &9) and *"Brain Freeze"* (pg.14 & 15). She believes that art should be uplifting. She strives to make each piece a positive experience for herself and those around her. She wrote and illustrated "The Adventures of Silly Tilly" and illustrated "Pricilla Pig's Culinary Crisis". Her art can be seen at The Uptown Gallery in Franklin, NC where she lives with her husband and their much loved Pomeranian, Sweetie.

Marilyn illustrated the beautiful paintings that are made to look like photographs in the story "Max's Wesser Bald Adventure" (pg. 10-12). She played an important role in the development of the Macon County Art Association and Uptown Gallery. Marilyn is a much loved resident of The Franklin House and continues to share her artwork, love and good humor with all those around her.

PUZZLE ANSWER SHEET

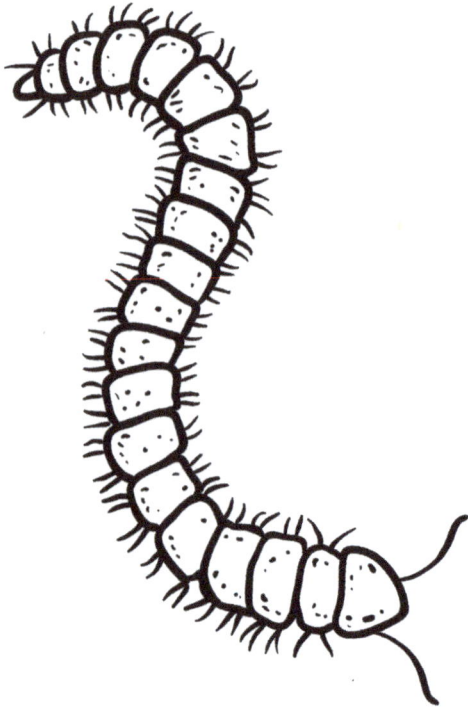

```
I B T M X Z X Y P M J A K S S J H C S C
E U U Z R D M X R X I D N U D Y Z I U R C
H N Z U H V O I I D S L K E F I R A O T
O Y S T S B N T M P N S L R E I L T C O T
T L R B P Y K L A U I O I R P J O F
H H N Y R V E T K G F S M P U C R E L
H Y C E N C Y Y I E T W Z W M A F P S C L
P C V U K O H R S U B G I S I C D S C A
B J N A T H B V S J L V S M N Q A E V M
C J W N P S M E I B F Z H N S C P V G A
O L A I R Z H A A P T S E D T U V T X A
T B M M D S Y C M R U H L P I S R U D A N
T R D A F C U I A Q H A L H N H X G E B
E H Z I U E P U N B H A B D C T R E A X
R U W E D N Z C G N I I I T M C A V C
C C Q B Y T A G U K L T N G W M H U N I
Y P S W I M M I N G N A D R K P U N S E T
Z M F I P T K P B M O T E O U S B I N I T
O B A B I E S K V U S B R O J F E N T F
O J C T C B L W I L D L I F E T E N M
```

HELLBENDER   MILLIPEDE   INSTINCT   SWIMMING

PRIMATES   WILDLIFE   CURATOR   DEFENSE

SIAMANG   HABITAT   SCIENCE   MONKEY

ANIMAL   CANINE   SHRIMP   BABIES

SCENT   LLAMA   BEAR   OTTER

DEER   ZOO

1. LLAAM = LLAMA
2. TROET = OTTER
3. BEAR = BEAR
4. YLIGOOB = BIOLOGY
5. CRVGNESEAS = SCAVENGERS
6. CTESN = SCENT
7. NRNNEVOIMET = ENVIRONMENT
8. IITSNTNC = INSTINCT
9. BTAIHAT = HABITAT
10. ILIFWEDL = WILDLIFE

MEMA
BY CLAIRE SUMINSKI

Cowee Sam

Cookbook
by Claire Suminski
and Susan Swedlund

Cowee Counting

Wee-Tee
The Farm Cat and Her "EE" Adventures

Meet Cowee Sam

Cowee Sam and the Swift Water Rescue
By Claire Suminski and

Cowee Sam
AND THE Scottish Highlands Games Adventure
By Claire Suminski and

Cowee Sam
and the Solar Eclipse

GO BACK-A ALPACA!
by Claire Suminski

Cowee Sam Rides Again!
By Claire Suminski and Annie Suminski

Cowee Sam and the Eagles' Nest
By Claire and Ann

Cowee Sam and the Special Delivery

Read Aloud
Animal Stories
For Families
Collected Claire Su
Illustra Susan Swedlund

Read Aloud
Animal Stories 2
For Families
Collected by Claire Suminski
Illustrated by Susan Swedlund and Friends

Suminski Family Books

FAITH, FAMILY, DILIGENCE, AND LOVE

Suminski Family Books Order Form
You may also order on-line at www.suminskifamilybooks.com

Cowee Sam Series $14.95 each

Cowee Sam
Cowee Sam and the Swift Water Rescue
Cowee Sam and the Solar Eclipse
Cowee Sam Rides Again!
Cowee Sam and the Scottish Highlands Games Adventure
Cowee Sam and the Eagles' Nest
Cowee Sam's Family Fun Cookbook
Cowee Sam and the Special Delivery

Reading is an Exciting Adventure Series $8.95 each

Meet Cowee Sam
Wee-Tee the Farm Cat and Her "EE' Adventure
Cowee Counting

We Survived the Eclipse!
Accounts of the 2017 Total Solar Eclipse in Franklin, NC and Surrounding Areas
$19.95

The Early Grade School Reading Series $11.95 each

Go Back-a Alpaca

Read Aloud Animal Stories for Families Series $14.95 each
Animal Stories 1
Animal Stories 2
Animal Stories 3

Please make checks out to **Suminski Family Books**

and send order to : 32 Jim Berry Road Franklin, NC 28734 or email order to: Claire@dometrics.com

Name_____

Address:_____

_____

Phone:_____   Email:_____

Name of Book:	# of Copies	Amount
Free Shipping		
~~Shipping: $2.50 for 1 book/$5.00 2-9 Books/10 or over ships free~~		
(Based on United Postal Service Media Rate)	shipping:	FREE
Total	Total:	

www.ingramcontent.com/pod-product-compliance
Lightning Source LLC
Chambersburg PA
CBHW042354030426
42336CB00029B/3480